NBS Guide to Tendering: for construction projects

Roland Finch

Published by ∩ЬＲ

About the author: Roland Finch, BSc. FRICS ACI.Arb, is one of NBS's technical authors. He is a chartered quantity surveyor with over 30 years' construction industry experience in both the public and private sectors.

Roland is a past consulting editor of *Croner's Management of Construction Projects*, and until 2010, was a member of the RICS QS and Construction Professional Group Board. He is also a Trustee of the RICS Education Trust.

Acknowledgement: The author and publisher are grateful for the editorial assistance of Richard Teale.

© RIBA Enterprises Ltd., 2011

Published by RIBA Publishing, 15 Bonhill Street, London EC2P 2EA

ISBN 978 1 85946 388 8

Stock code 74338

British Library Cataloguing in Publications Data
A catalogue record for this book is available from the British Library.

Publisher: Steven Cross
Commissioning Editor: Matthew Thompson
Project Editor: Gray Publishing
Designed and typeset by Gray Publishing, Tunbridge Wells
Printed and bound by Polstar Wheatons

RIBA Publishing is part of RIBA Enterprises Ltd.
www.ribaenterprises.com

Contents

Foreword

In late 2009, the UK's Office of Fair Trading (OFT) completed an investigation into bid-rigging in breach of 'the Chapter I prohibition' of the Competition Act 1998 involving over 100 construction companies. This Part of the Act is concerned with restrictive practices that have the effect of distorting, restricting or preventing competition, meaning that one party has an unfair advantage, with the result that prices are driven up; while other organisations may not be able to compete for work.

The penalties imposed by the Competition Act 1998 reflect the importance attached by the government to misdemeanours of this nature. The Act permits the OFT to levy fines of up to 10% of a company's annual UK turnover for every year in which a violation has taken place up to a maximum of three years.

The result of this investigation was the imposition of fines totalling £129.2 million on 103 construction firms found to have colluded with competitors in breach of 'the Chapter I prohibition'.

One of the key findings of the investigation was the lack of clear rules concerning how the procurement process was managed.

Who this guide is for

This guide is aimed at clients, architects, surveyors, designers, engineers, project managers and others who are involved directly in the management of procurement and tendering for construction works. It is also intended to serve as a useful reference for contractors, suppliers and subcontractors who experience part of that process at different stages.

1 Introduction and scope

Tendering is the process by which bids are invited from interested contractors to carry out specific packages of construction work. The purpose of this guide is to set out rules and procedures which will encourage best practice in tendering, and so provide good value for all parties involved in the process. It attempts to fill some of the gaps left following the withdrawal from print of previously published codes, particularly those by the National Joint Consultative Committee for Building (NJCC), Joint Contracts Tribunal (JCT) and others, which formed the industry standard (see 'Historical background' following). In doing so, it proposes adoption and observance of the key values of fairness, clarity, simplicity and accountability, as well as reinforcing the idea that the apportionment of risk to the party best placed to assess and manage it is fundamental to the success of a project.

This guide is relevant to projects of all sizes and values. However, for low value or straightforward projects some of the procedures may be applied less formally, although, of course, the legal requirements must always be observed.

When organisations or individuals wish to have a new facility, or carry out refurbishment or maintenance of an existing facility, they will be involved in some form of procurement. There are a variety of different methods for procuring this new facility, not all of which involve construction as a solution. A complete new building may be purchased, for example, or existing space may be leased. It is assumed, therefore, that reference to later parts of this document will only be required once the decision has been taken – and recorded – to proceed with the construction option.

The two most commonly used methods of tendering are single-stage selective tendering or two-stage selective tendering. Both involve the invitation of tenders from firms on a pre-approved or *ad hoc* list, chosen because they meet certain minimum standards in general criteria such as financial standing, experience, capability and competence. The competition element of the tender is provided on the basis of price and quality. The main difference between the two is that in the two-stage process, the contractor becomes involved in the planning of the project at an earlier stage, so the tenders are submitted on the basis of minimal information, and in the second stage the employer's team will develop the precise specification in conjunction with the preferred tenderer. This method is favoured in more complex projects, where the contractor may have significant design input.

This guide is concerned with the activities involved in single-stage selective tendering in the UK, although there is also discussion of other methodologies. The processes described concentrate mainly on the use of hard-copy documents, but can be used with electronic or online methods, where they are compatible with legislative requirements. Indeed, some of the timescales prescribed by European procurement legislation may be shortened if electronic communications are used. While it is specifically directed at the activities associated with the management of stages F, G and H (Preconstruction) in the *RIBA architects' plan of work*, it is expected that the principles will extend beyond that scope.

It is worth remembering that every activity in the tendering process has a time and cost implication. It makes economic sense, therefore, not to overburden the participants with unnecessary information requirements, and to concentrate on those which are relevant to the work which is to be undertaken. Faced with competing financial pressures, most contractors will carry out their own assessment of the jobs they wish to tender for, and will be less inclined to bid for those where the procedures involved are perceived as overly complicated or onerous. Also, since preparation costs are included in their overheads, these will ultimately be passed on, in the form of higher prices. Preparation of this information will also be reflected in higher consultancy costs for the employer's team.

The principle of tendering is to ensure that true competition is achieved, as it is evaluated by applying certain criteria. These criteria may be expressed in terms of financial matters, comprising a simple assessment relating to tender sums, or more complex financial evaluation, including consideration of projected costs over the life cycle of the completed project. It could also address other non-financial factors such as time and proposed methods or levels of capability; or sometimes a mixture of both – collectively referred to as a 'quality/price balance' or 'matrix'.

European legislation describes this concept as the assessment of the most 'economically advantageous' option. In order for this to be achieved, however, each tenderer should be able to bid on an equal basis, meaning that they must receive the same information – and most importantly that this information should be sufficient in content and accuracy to allow them to properly assess the implications and bid accordingly.

In the public sector, failure to follow fair and transparent procedures can lead to automatic challenges to a subsequent contract. This may result in damages, or the contract being set aside, or both. While this may not apply equally in the private sector, it is sensible to adhere to these principles, if only to make the process itself easier to follow.

It is important to ensure in any event that any discussions which take place are conducted fairly and recorded accurately. The Fraud Act 2006 defines a number of activities which can be described as fraud, while the Bribery Act 2010 can penalise a company whose employees engage in bribery, if the company does not have adequate procedures in place to prevent it.

Terms used in this guide

For ease of use, the following terms to describe certain roles and activities have been adopted:

- Participants: The persons or organisations involved in the tendering process.
- Employer: The person or organisation in whose name the work is being commissioned. This includes the terms building owner, buyer, client, purchaser, etc.
- Tenderer: The person or organisation bidding for the work. This includes the terms builder, service provider, supplier, as the context allows. It is intended that once a

tender is accepted and a formal contract is executed, the successful tenderer will become the 'contractor' for the purposes of that contract.

- Contract administrator (CA): The person or organisation administering the tendering process. This is irrespective of any other title or designation they may have. The CA role is commonly undertaken by an architect or surveyor. (Note: once a contract is executed, the CA may also be appointed to carry out some functions under that contract. The role and title will then be defined separately by the relevant contract documents.)

Legislation

For public sector construction contracts above a specified value (which is recalculated annually but is typically around €5 million for 'Works Contracts'), tenders must be invited and contracts awarded in accordance with Directive 71/305/EEC (as amended by Directive 89/440/EEC), implemented in England, Wales and Northern Ireland by The Public Contracts Regulations SI 2006/5 (these regulations are separately enacted in Scotland). 'Public contracting authorities' within the meaning of the Regulations are responsible for ensuring that their tender and award procedures for works contracts comply with the provisions of the Regulations or subsequent legislation. In these instances, the requirements of the legislation will take precedence over the recommendations of this guide.

Where specific legislation applies to the procurement of particular goods, works or services, the provisions of this guide will be qualified by the supplementary procedures specified in that legislation.

Freedom of information

The Freedom of Information Act 2000 applies to any request for recorded information made to a public authority. Section 8 of the Act notes that requests for information may be in any form and do not need to mention the Freedom of Information Act. They must, however, be in writing, give the applicant's name and a return address and describe the information that is requested. Disclosure of environmental information may also be required under the Environmental Information Regulations.

If the Act does apply to any of the project participants, or others associated with the project, then information generated or held as part of the procurement process could be the subject of a request. It may be necessary, therefore, to advise tenderers of how this procedure will apply to them.

Historical background

The NJCC was set up in 1954, after public attention had been focused on the importance of selective, as opposed to indiscriminate, tendering. The original constituent bodies during the first two decades of the NJCC were the RIBA, Royal Institution of Chartered Surveyors (RICS) and Building Employers Confederation (BEC) (then the National Federation of Building Trades Employers, NFBTE). Following the publication of the Banwell Report, *The placing and management of contracts for building and civil engineering work,* the Association of Consulting Engineers, the Federation of Building Specialist Contractors and the Confederation of Associations of Specialist Engineering Contractors joined the NJCC in the early 1970s.

For many years, the procedures for Tendering were enshrined in various industry codes of procedures. The most prominent was the NJCC *Code of procedure for single stage competitive tendering.* It was first published in 1959, with the last edition in 1996. Following the demise of the NJCC, some of the principles of its code were incorporated into Practice Note 6 (Series 2); *Main contract tendering,* published by RIBA Enterprises for JCT in 1999.

A note on sustainability

BS 8900:2006, *Guidance for managing sustainable development,* defines sustainable development as 'an enduring balanced approach to economic activity, environmental responsibility and social progress'. There are a number of shared objectives between this definition, as it is generally applied to the construction process, and the overriding principle of achieving value for money. Examples include:

• Minimising use of resources and reducing waste.
• Minimising the negative impacts of those resources on public health and the environment.
• Fair, ethical and transparent treatment of suppliers and the supply chain.
• Support for communities and businesses.
• Encouraging positive outcomes for the environment, economy and society.

BS 8903:2010, *Principles and framework for procuring sustainably – guide,* declares that this approach: 'allows organizations to meet their needs for goods, services, works and utilities in a way that achieves value for money on a whole-life basis ...'.

It goes on to say:

> Sustainable procurement should consider the environmental, social and economic consequences of: design; non-renewable material use; manufacture and production methods; logistics; service delivery; use; operation; maintenance; reuse; recycling options; disposal; and suppliers' capabilities to address these consequences throughout the supply chain.

It makes sense, therefore, to integrate sustainable practices into the procurement process. Increasing numbers of employers have developed policies on sustainability, and these should be reflected in any procurement strategy.

2 Procurement strategy

A sensible procurement strategy and approach to tendering is crucial in achieving a successful project. The Office of Government Commerce (OGC) Achieving Excellence in Construction procurement document *Procurement and contract strategies* notes:

> ... the procurement strategy identifies the best way of achieving the objectives of the project and value for money, taking account of the risks and constraints, leading to decisions about the funding mechanism and asset ownership for the project. The aim of a procurement strategy is to achieve the optimum balance of risk, control and funding for a particular project ...
>
> The procurement route delivers the procurement strategy. It includes the contract strategy that will best meet the client's needs. An integrated procurement route ensures that design, construction, operation and maintenance are considered as a whole; it also ensures that the delivery team work together as an integrated project team.

Since 2000, the UK government's general policy has been that construction projects should be procured by one of three recommended routes (private finance initiative, prime contracting or design and build). However, 'traditional' procurement, with a contractual arrangement between an employer and contractor but with a third-party consultant carrying out design and contract administration services, is still widely used in both the public and private sectors.

The employer should have developed a strategy which covers procurement of construction works. This can vary from a simple record of the decision to proceed with construction, to a complex model with many options and decisions.

Points to consider include:

- What are the likely risks to be encountered in terms of project delivery. Are these being allocated to the party best placed to deal with them?
- Are there any issues associated with funding, such as timing of availability or restrictions on its spending?
- Is there any specific legislation applicable to the project or the work [such as European Union (EU) rules, Construction (Design and Management) Regulations SI 2007/320, etc.]?
- Do potential tenderers have capability, capacity and motivation to carry out the work?
- How is the work best controlled?
- How is the work best packaged?
- Is there an optimum contract duration/programme?
- Are there any sustainability/environmental issues?
- Are there any framework agreements in place with suitable contractors?
- Are there any supply agreements in place for specific products or services?

- What are the contract management options?
- What are the pricing/information requirements?
- Are there any key performance indicators?

There may be elements of the strategy which are relevant to the tender process and will allow tenderers to better understand what is expected of them. The choice of options depends on the nature and objectives of the project and the route that offers the best potential for the delivery of value for money. Some information, however, may be commercially sensitive, so caution should be exercised when deciding which parts should be made available and it could be that an abridged version is required for this purpose.

A description should be included explaining how copies of any documents may be obtained, or arrangements for their inspection.

Public sector bodies may be obliged to comply with a standard framework such as that produced by the OGC (www.ogc.gov.uk).

Contract choice

It is strongly recommended that a standard form of building contract is used for any subsequent construction work, and that it is appropriate to the type of procurement being envisaged – so that if, for example, completion in sections or contractor's design is envisaged, the correct form is used. Several publishers produce forms for use in a variety of situations, and while it is sometimes tempting to make amendments to the terms and conditions, it should be recognised that these have been developed with the intention of fairly apportioning risk and responsibility. In the case of the JCT they have the further advantage of cross-industry consensus in their drafting.

For guidance on contract choice, see RIBA Publishing's *Which Contract?*.

Procurement team and timetable

Where appropriate, give details of who is to be in the project procurement team, and what their roles and responsibilities are. The main events and their dates should also be listed. These should all be cross-referenced to a prior information notice, where one is produced (see 'Advance information' following).

Guidance on the European procurement rules, including details of the financial thresholds and typical timetables is contained in the OGC document: *Introduction to the EU procurement rules: OGC guidance* (www.ogc.gov.uk).

3 Establishing a tender list

The purpose of establishing a list is to be confident that each contractor chosen to tender will be able to meet specified eligibility criteria, primarily the ability to carry out successfully the work which is subject to tender, if appointed. The competitive element of tendering is then restricted to the tendering process itself.

Lists of prospective tenderers may be compiled in several different ways, depending on the type of work being procured and a number of factors surrounding its execution. It is important to ensure the method chosen is appropriate to the procurement strategy and proposed contractual arrangements.

There may be particular eligibility criteria which the employer values above others, but it should be noted that, under EU law, no discrimination is allowed against 'economic operators' from other member states. The scope of this legislation is quite broad and can range from simple things like use of a particular language in documents to requirements to 'use only local labour or materials' in specifications. The British Standards Institution (BSi) has produced a standard, PAS 91:2010, *Construction related procurement – Prequalification questionnaires*.

EU legislation requires that set procedures and timetables are adhered to, depending on the procurement route to be followed. It recognises these commonly used designations:

- Open – available to all applicants who express an interest following an initial notice.
- Restricted – available to pre-qualified applicants.
- Negotiated or competitive dialogue.
- Design competition.

Advance information

It makes sense to advise prospective tenderers that a construction project is in development. This enables them to decide whether they want to bid for the work, and allows them to express an interest, where appropriate. The nature and content of this information will depend on the project itself, and the particular requirements of the employer, in particular, the extent to which it is governed by its own constitutional rules, regulations and policies. For public sector contracts, the procedures are normally governed by legislation.

A prior information notice is required by The Public Contracts Regulations SI 2006/5 for projects which exceed certain financial thresholds. This is a public announcement giving advance warning of likely projects for which tenders are to be invited.

For public works, the form, location and timing of the notice will normally be prescribed. Subject to some exclusions, the Regulations require the notice to be published 'as soon as possible after the decision authorising the programme of public works contracts or framework agreements for the carrying out of work or works' and it must be placed in the *Official Journal of the European Union*. For other projects, however, it could take the form of a simple advertisement in a suitable trade publication. Tenderers should be given details of where and when the information may be found and draw attention to significant points listed in it.

Pre-qualification

The objective of selection is to make a list of firms, any one of which could be entrusted with the job. If this is achieved, then the final choice of contractor will be simplified.

Pre-qualification should not be confused with two-stage tendering. In the former, a tenderer must prove its capability before being invited to submit a tender. (In the latter, the submitted tenders are partially evaluated against a set of criteria with which they must conform before proceeding to the next stage where they are evaluated against a further set of criteria.) Prospective tenderers may be invited to pre-qualify for a single project, or for a range of projects, if the employer is intending to undertake an extended programme of work.

Indicate if there is no requirement for pre-qualification, because, for example, it has already been received, or relevant information will be required as part of the tender. If pre-qualification is required, describe the procedure to be followed or specify by reference to the appropriate document.

The pre-qualification questionnaire

The purpose of a pre-qualification questionnaire is to simplify tendering processes by:

- Setting basic eligibility criteria for prospective tenderers, thus reducing the likelihood of non-compliant tenders being submitted by underqualified or under-resourced organisations.
- Saving time and effort by reducing the need for unnecessary repetition of information for each tender.

It is often the case that a single contractor is capable of undertaking a variety of different work types but it is preferable they should not have to duplicate things like 'corporate' particulars, which will also need to be checked, to support every tender. Ideally, all the information submitted *with the tender* should be project specific, and evaluated as such.

The Public Contracts Regulations SI 2006/5 generally requires questions to be restricted to the following headings:

- Structure of the tendering organisation.
- Financial capability of the tendering organisation.
- Technical capability of the tendering organisation.
- References.

The headings are capable of fairly broad interpretation, and represent the opportunity to enquire into the organisation's capability and the extent to which it matches the employer's own aspirations in a number of different areas, including:

- General experience, skill and reputation in the area in question, identifying recent examples of building at the required rate of completion over a comparable contract period.
- Technical and management structure including the control of subcontractors for the type of contract envisaged.
- Competence and resources in respect of statutory health and safety requirements.
- Approach to quality assurance.
- Environmental credentials.
- Capacity at the relevant time.

This can be done through a questionnaire, and it may be appropriate to seek confidential references from third parties. It may also be appropriate, in some cases, to invite applicants to interview in order to clarify particular responses to the questionnaire.

Directions should be given of where and how applications can be made, together with any conditions for completion and return of information.

Model and template questionnaire forms are available from a variety of sources, such as consultants, professional institutions or government departments, while the employer may have their own. The OGC produces one, available from its website (www.ogc.gov.uk).

Tender lists may be compiled for a specific project, or in the form of an approved list for a number of projects. For straightforward or one-off projects, it may be simpler and more cost-effective to require this information to be submitted with the tender, and form part of the tender evaluation, but it is important to allow sufficient time in the process for this activity to take place. References from third parties, for example, can often take some time to arrive.

Some employers or consultants maintain their own 'approved' tender lists, where, following a separate pre-qualification exercise, contractors are classified according to the type or category of work they are permitted to undertake, financial thresholds, geographical location, or a mixture of these. These lists should be reviewed periodically to exclude firms whose performance has been unsatisfactory, and to allow the introduction of suitable additional firms.

As an alternative, lists may be compiled and accredited by a third party, such as Constructionline (www.constructionline.co.uk). This method may be more appropriate if the employer does not have the necessary expertise in house, or it is costly to implement for a single project. One disadvantage, however, is that the process is unlikely to be tailored to the specific requirements of the project.

If this route is chosen, details should be provided of the 'third-party' assessor, and describe any requirements of approval for a particular work type or category. Where there are known procedures to be followed for inclusion in the approved list, these should also be stated.

A short-list of suitable organisations for the project under consideration should be drawn up using one of the means described.

The larger the tender list becomes, the greater will be the potential cost of abortive tendering, and this will be reflected in higher prices. Regard should also be paid to the amount of work demanded of tenderers in order to formulate their bids. Where this involves extensive quantification, specification, specialisation and/or calculation, the number on the project list should not be excessive. Historically, most codes of procedure have recommended a maximum of six tenderers, with fewer where the work is specialist in nature.

It may be advisable to retain details of one or two further prospective tenderers in case those invited do not accept the preliminary enquiry. All tenderers should be advised of the number of tenders invited, but it should not be necessary to share precise details of other invitees. However, in the public sector where the EU 'open' procedure is chosen, there is no specified limit, all qualifying tenderers should be invited to bid.

Establishment of willingness to tender: the preliminary enquiry

Once the list of prospective tenderers is compiled, it is prudent and courteous to check whether they are still interested in competing for the work.

It is possible that, due to changes in circumstances, some of the preferred tenderers are no longer willing or able to comply with the tendering timetable or requirements. They may no longer have the capacity to carry out a contract at the relevant time, or it could be they have made a commercial decision to move away from a particular market or location. In order that tenderers may be able to finally anticipate demands on their tendering staff, enquiries should be made to establish whether they intend to submit a bid in advance of sending the formal tender invitation. One of the major problems, which initiated the OGC investigation outlined earlier, was the increasing practice of 'cover pricing'. This occurs when a tenderer finds itself unable to submit a bid, but rather than prejudice the possibility of subsequent work for an employer, will submit a bid which has not been properly programmed or quantified, excepting that it is calculated so as *not* to be the lowest or most acceptable. Unfortunately, in some thankfully rare circumstances, tenderers have colluded with each other in order to ensure that this was the case; in extreme occasions bribes were offered to ensure that the outcome of the tendering process was artificially controlled.

It is a far more satisfactory outcome for the tenderer to be able to simply decline, but they must be reassured that this will not have any negative repercussions, particularly where the employer will also be under pressure to demonstrate that competition has been achieved, and one of the measures of this is the number of tenders received.

It is essential that all the points itemised following are addressed in this preliminary enquiry. The omission of relevant information may deter contractors from tendering, or lead to problems later.

The preliminary enquiry should include details of anticipated:

- Employer and consultants.
- Project description.
- Description of the works and location.
- Proposed form of contract and amendments thereto.

- Pricing method.
- Approximate estimate of cost.
- Proposed commencement and completion dates of the works.
- Tendering dates.
- Number of tenders to be invited.
- Basis of tender evaluation.
- Health and safety details – CDM co-ordinator, principal contractor, planning period (if relevant).
- Requirements for bonds, guarantees and warranties (and beneficiaries, if known).
- Other significant requirements.
- Date, address and format for reply to enquiry.
- The date on which the enquiry was issued, details of a unique reference where possible and an explanation of where the information may be inspected or further copies obtained.

Tenderers' attention should be specifically drawn to any alterations to be made to the standard form of contract and, where appropriate, reasons should be given, so that the implications of such alterations may be considered by tenderers prior to acceptance of the invitation to tender. This will minimise the risk of subsequent queries which could result in an extension of the tender period.

Some of this information will duplicate that which would otherwise be included in the tender documents. It may be tempting to refer to the enquiry rather than reproduce information for tendering purposes. However, while there should not be inconsistencies between the preliminary enquiry and the tender information, the tender documents should comprise all the information necessary to prepare a tender, so it may make sense to include a further copy of the preliminary enquiry with the invitation to tender.

The Public Contracts Regulations SI 2006/5 stipulate a maximum period of 52 days between preliminary enquiry and return of tenders.

The specification

The Construction Project Information Committee (CPIC) is formed from representatives of the major industry institutions which ensures that the guidance it provides has a solid foundation within all branches of the industry. It is responsible for providing best practice guidance on the content, form and preparation of construction production information, and making sure this best practice is disseminated throughout the UK construction industry.

The CPIC Code of Practice, *Production information: a code of procedure for the construction industry*, defines production specification as: 'written information prepared by the design team for use by the construction team, the main purpose of which is to define the products to be used, the quality of work, any performance requirements, and the conditions under which the work is to be executed.' Part of this specification will necessarily include the means by which the work is to be subject to tender.

It is of key importance that the specification is clearly defined, as omissions or conflicts will serve to delay progress and increase costs. In particular, if the contractor is expected to carry out design as part of the contract, the employer's requirements are unambiguous and properly developed.

If it is intended that the design is to be developed as part of the tendering process with a preferred bidder, then single-stage tendering may not be appropriate and consideration should be given to alternative methods, such as a two-stage process.

4 The tender rules

These rules form the basis of how the formal process will be handled and managed, together with instructions to tenderers and details of how the evaluation model will be applied. Other points which should be addressed include:

- Details of the documents which form part of the tender package.
- Guidance on how documents are to be completed – pricing and other insertions.
- Instructions on information to be returned with the tender.
- Instructions on how tender documents are to be returned; destination, timing, format, etc.
- Key dates for tender assessment – identifying when a decision is likely to be made.

The rules will normally form part of the specification itself, or be contained in the invitation to tender. Care should be taken to ensure that there is no duplication or conflict between the two documents. An example invitation to tender is given in the Appendix.

Worked example

The following is a worked example, using clauses in the format of the National Building Specification (NBS) – the UK industry standard master specification system. These should be refined to suit the particular principles which apply to the specific project procedures.

Preliminaries clauses	£	p
A90 TENDERING		
THE TENDER RULES		
110 ACCEPTANCE OF TENDER • Assurance: Nothing contained in this document or its application should be inferred to guarantee that a tender will be recommended for acceptance or be accepted, or that reasons for non-acceptance will be given. • Compliance: Failure to comply with the conditions set out in this document may result in tenders being rejected at the sole discretion of the employer. • Costs: No liability is accepted for costs incurred in the preparation of a tender.		

Preliminaries clauses	£	p
120 PRELIMINARY ENQUIRY • Details: See letter reference H5a dated 13th March 2011.		
130 TENDERS TO BE INVITED • Maximum number: Six.		
130 PROJECT TEAM AGREEMENT • Document: Location: reference PTA/1 enclosed with the tender documents. • Execution: Complete and return with the tender.		

Details: Describe, e.g. the date on which the enquiry was issued, details of a unique reference where possible and explain where the information may be inspected or further copies available. The Public Contracts Regulations SI 2006/5 stipulate a maximum period of 52 days between preliminary enquiry and return of tenders.

All tenderers should be advised of the number of tenders invited, but it should not be necessary to share precise details of other invitees.

It may be advisable to retain the details of one or two further prospective tenderers in case those invited do not.

Document location: Describe where the document may be inspected and completed or insert, e.g. included with the tender documents.

Execution: Give directions on how it is to be completed and returned. insert, e.g. with the tender within X days of request.

Preliminaries clauses	£	p

140 FRAMEWORK AGREEMENTS
• Framework agreements:
  – In place with the following suppliers/subcontractors.
  – Details: None in place.		

150 TENDER PROCESS • Details: Included in the preliminary enquiry.		
160 THE INVITATION TO TENDER • Form: Document H6a dated 7th June 2011. • Location: Included with the tender documents.		
165 TENDER ACCEPTANCE Period: Tenders must remain open for acceptance, unless previously withdrawn, for a minimum of 13 weeks from the date of return of tenders.		

170 THE TENDER DOCUMENTS
• Comprise:
  – Drawings listed on issue sheet TD/1/dated 7th June 2011.
  – Specification.
  – Form of tender.
  – Appendices A–D inclusive.
• Format: Hard copy.
• Number of copies: Two copies of all documents.		

180 TENDER QUERIES • Queries or discrepancies in the tender documents: – Notification requirements: Give notice in writing to the issuing authority or the architect (with a copy to the quantity surveyor) as soon as possible and not less than 10 working days before the date for return of tenders.		

Give details of agreements which are in place relating to the supply of products to be used in the project which is the subject of the tender.

Give an overview of the principal dates. This should be cross-referenced with the preliminary enquiry (see clause 120) or, should cover the same content headings, if details are not provided elsewhere.

Preliminaries clauses	£	p

190 GENERAL INSTRUCTIONS
• General: Failure to comply with instructions may lead to rejection of a tender without further consideration.
• Qualifications: Do not amend or alter documents without written instruction.
• Information supplied with the tender: Prepare in the format required.
• Handling of tender documents: In accordance with the invitation to tender.
 	
200 CONFIDENTIALLITY
• Disclosure: Do not reveal details of parts of the tender or supporting documents (except for the necessary purposes of preparing that tender) without the employer's express written permission.
 	
210 PRICING
• Generally: Price and extend each item individually as instructed. Do not group items together.
• Currency: Pounds sterling.
 	
220 SITE VISIT
• Before tendering: Ascertain the nature of the site, access thereto and local conditions and restrictions likely to affect the execution of the works.
  – Arrangements for visit: By appointment with the CA.
 	
230 RETURN OF TENDER
• Return of tender:
  – Destination: In accordance with instructions given in the tender invitation.
  – Inability to tender: Advise immediately if the work as defined in the tender documents cannot be tendered.
  – Relevant parts of the work: Define those parts, stating reasons for the inability to tender.
 	
TENDER ASSESSMENT
 	
310 ASSESSMENT
• Number of tenders to be assessed in detail: All received.
  – Assessment criteria: Most economically advantageous.
• Assessment model details: As document A/S Mod 1, available for inspection on request from the CA.
 	
• Alternative tenders: Not accepted.
  – Basis: N/A.		

Preliminaries clauses	£	p
320 ERRORS – RESOLUTION • Arithmetic: Tender price will prevail. An opportunity will be given to confirm the tender or withdraw. – Corrections: An endorsement will be added to the priced documents indicating that rates or prices (excluding preliminaries, contingencies prime cost and provisional sums) inserted therein will be adjusted in the same proportion as the corrected total differs from that stated incorrectly. • Technical: The tender is deemed to meet or exceed the requirements of the tender documents. Amendment of the tender to reflect this will not constitute a variation and no claim for additional costs will be accepted. NOTIFICATION OF RESULTS 400 NOTIFICATION TO TENDERERS • Notification: – Details: Results will be notified to all tenderers and published on the employer's website no later than 15 weeks following the return of tenders.		

5 Tender assessment

Tenders should be opened as soon as possible after the time for receipt of tenders. The invitation to tender and the tender rules should identify the number of submissions to be examined in detail; this will depend on the complexity of the assessment model which should be appropriate to the contract envisaged, and will have been made available for inspection. Where price is the chief assessment criterion, it should be easy to identify the lowest tender, but where other measures are included, a ranking may not become apparent until detailed examination has taken place.

The specification should identify the documentation and supporting information which should accompany the tender and that which may be requested subsequently as part of the assessment. Some of this information will not be needed unless the tender is subject to detailed scrutiny, so as to avoid abortive work on the part of tenderers, but it should be made clear to them when this information is required to be submitted, and they should be informed that failure to comply with this requirement may render the tender liable to rejection.

Detailed assessment

Once it has been decided to examine tenders in detail, and all supporting documents have been submitted, the assessment will take place in two principal stages.

Stage 1

A basic check that everything requested has been submitted and those submissions are complete; if a pricing document is included, it should be subject to an arithmetic and technical check.

Errors discovered during this process may be dealt with in one of two ways. Tenderers should be advised which alternative will apply:

- Alternative 1: Tender price will prevail. The tender is deemed to comply in all technical respects with the specified requirements. An opportunity will be given to confirm the tender or withdraw, and the documents will be endorsed to reconcile the error.
- Alternative 2: The tenderer will be given an opportunity of confirming their offer or amending it to correct genuine errors. If correction means that the tender is no longer eligible for acceptance under the selected assessment criteria, then it will be disqualified from that process.

Stage 2

Depending on the complexity of the job and evaluation model to be used, there may be a separate evaluation looking in more depth at individual pricing proposals and method statement responses. The purpose of this is to identify variances from the anticipated responses predicted by the project team, and to allow application of the evaluation model itself. This will sometimes take the form of a separate evaluation report, carried out by a quantity surveyor or architect from the project team, or a specialist in the area being examined. It could be that as part of this process clarification is sought from individual tenderers, but it is also important to remember that all tenderers should be treated fairly and equally.

It is also essential to ensure that the tender satisfies all aspects of the specified requirements, in particular with regard to aspects of health and safety, and the requirements for competence prescribed by the Construction (Design and Management) Regulations SI 2007/320. Further information in this regard is available from the Health and Safety Executive (www.hse.gov.uk).

Once evaluation is complete, a report should be prepared, and this would normally include a recommendation for acceptance of one of the tenders. It is possible, however, that the lowest tender may still exceed the employer's budget, or be unacceptable for another technical reason, such as proposing a method of working which cannot be accommodated. (This would be rare, because it would be unusual for it not to be anticipated by the project team.) If this is the case, the employer will have to decide how to proceed. There are a number of alternatives, including:

- Increase the budget or review acceptability of proposed methods.
- Negotiated reduction of the tender – sometimes referred to as 'value engineering' (although probably not correct in the purest sense of the term).
- Abandon the tendering exercise, or repeat it with a different scope.

Advice and guidance as to the most appropriate alternative should be sought from the project team, and it should be documented and recorded for future reference. None of these decisions should be taken lightly, as there could be significant time and cost consequences, as well as affecting the tenderer's willingness to take part.

Confidentiality

It is important to maintain strict confidentiality while assessment is undertaken. It may also be necessary to co-ordinate with a statutory timescale for this process.

6 The contract award

Tender acceptance

Under the law of England and Wales, an offer may be withdrawn at any time before acceptance, although there are exceptions. Under the law of Scotland, an undertaking to keep a tender open for a specified period is usually binding.

Tenderers should be advised how long their tender is to remain open for acceptance. By identifying a precise period, tenderers can make a proper assessment of the documentation and circumstances. This should not be so unreasonably long or short as to make it unviable, but should allow adequate time that corresponds with any timetables given in the prior information notice.

The submission of an unqualified tender allows it to be accepted by the employer (following the principles set out in the case of *Carlill* v. *The Carbolic Smokeball Company Ltd*. [1893] 1 QB 256, [1892] EWCA Civ 1). However, care must be taken to ensure that all documentation required by the tender rules is submitted before this takes place – in particular such things as documentary evidence of insurances, and those relating to statutory health and safety requirements. If the contractor is to undertake any design work, there may also be development control procedures to observe.

Certain terms may be implied into contracts. The Sale of Goods Act 1979, the Supply of Goods and Services Act 1982 and/or the Unfair Contract Terms Act 1977 (as amended) contain terms which can be implied into all contracts for the sale of goods and services, primarily for the protection of those employers who may also be defined as 'consumers' for the purposes of the legislation.

Written contracts must be executed in accordance with specific requirements, otherwise, they will not be legally enforceable. There are different procedures which apply in England, Wales and Scotland. If there is any doubt, then appropriate legal advice should always be sought.

Once the tendering procedure has been successfully concluded, it will be necessary to complete a formal contract with the successful tenderer.

The Public Contracts Regulations SI 2006/5 require the posting of a contract award notice, within a set period, usually 48 days, of the actual award. However, the regulations also require the inclusion of a 'standstill' period during which time unsuccessful tenderers may request a further 'debrief' before the contract is entered into.

A note on contract administration

The scope of this guide ends at the point of contract formation, and does not deal in detail with the procedures after a tender has been accepted. It should be noted, however, that once the contract has been entered into, both parties will have rights, duties and obligations. The various standard forms of building contract set out a number of procedures and processes which must be observed, usually with the assistance of a 'third-party' consultant to oversee and administer, monitor performance and deal with change.

It is also useful to have regular project meetings to ensure that everything is going according to plan and to solve any problems as they arise, and a review at the end of each stage in the procurement process in order to identify areas for improvement.

'NBS Contract Administrator' is a software tool which provides extensive guidance and a number of template forms which will assist with this task.

Appendix

Standard letters

1. Preliminary invitation to tender

We are preparing a list of tenderers for constructing the works (description attached) under the JCT Standard Building Contract SBC05. We draw your attention to the option clauses which will apply. Any amendments will be set out in the tender documents.

If you wish to be invited to tender on this basis you must agree to submit *a bona fide* tender in accordance with the relevant published procedure notes and guidance on the selected method of tendering, and you must not divulge your tender price to any person or body before the time for submitting tenders. When the contract has been signed, we will send all those who tendered a list of the tenderers and prices.

Please reply to this letter by [date]. Your inclusion in our preliminary list does not guarantee that you will receive a formal invitation to tender, nor will your opportunities for tendering for future work be prejudiced if you do not wish to tender this time.

a.   Job:
b.   Employer:
c.   Architect:
d.   Quantity Surveyor:
e.   Consultants:
f.   Location of site: [enclose site plan]
g.   General description of the work:
h.   Approximate cost range £ .... to £ ....
i.   Listed (named) sub-contractors for major items:
j.   Form of contract [which edition, amendments, supplements].
k.   Fluctuations [if applicable]: Clause 4.21 and Schedule 7.
      Option to apply .... [A, B or C].

      Percentage addition to Option A paragraph A.12, or Option B paragraph B.13 [if applicable]:
      .... %.

l.   The contract is to be executed as a deed/simple contract*.
m.   Anticipated date for possession is ....
n.   Period for completing the works is ....
o.   Approximate date for dispatch of tender documents is ....
p.   Tender period is .... weeks.
q.   Tender to remain open for .... weeks.
r.   Liquidated damages: Anticipated value £ .... per ....
s.   Details of bond/guarantee requirements:

* Particular conditions applying to this contract.

2. Invitation to Tender under JCT SBC 05 with Bills of Quantities

We note that you wish to tender for these works.

We enclose:

- Two copies of the bill(s) of quantities.
- Two copies of the location drawings, component drawings, dimension drawings and information schedules.
- An addressed envelope in which to return the tender.
- Copies of relevant advance orders.

The completed form of tender, sealed in the envelope provided, should reach this office not later than 12 noon on [date].

Please note that:

1. Drawings and details may be inspected at [address].
2. The site may be inspected by arrangement with [name] at this office.
3. Tendering procedures will be in accordance with the relevant method of tendering.
4. Any queries should be raised with [name] at this office.
5. The building owner reserves the right to accept any tender from those submitted or to refuse all.

Please confirm that you have received this letter and enclosures and that you are prepared to tender in accordance with these instructions.

[Response]

We have read the conditions of contract and Bills of Quantities delivered to us and have examined the drawings referred to in them.

We offer to execute and complete in accordance with the conditions of contract the whole of the works described for the sum of:

£ .... (and in words) ....
....

within .... weeks from the date of site possession.

This tender remains open for consideration for .... days from the date fixed for submitting tenders.

We agree to provide a bond as required by the employer and name the following:

1 ....

2 ....

(assurance/guarantee societies/banks) as sureties, who are willing to be bound jointly and severally by us to the employer in the sum of £ .... for the performance of this contract. The amount included in the tender sum to cover the provision of a bond is £................................

Signed: ....   For: ....

3. Letter to successful tenderer

We are pleased to inform you that your tender for these works was the most acceptable. The priced documents are now being examined by the quantity surveyor and the construction phase Health and Safety Plan by the planning supervisor. [delete if not applicable]

We will write to you again when the examination has been completed.

4. Letter notifying unsuccessful tenderers

The tenders were opened on [date]. We regret to have to inform you that your tender was not successful. In due course we will send you a full list of tenderers and tendered prices.

Thank you for tendering. Although you have been unsuccessful this time, this will not prejudice your opportunities of tendering for our work in the future.

5. Letter notifying tender results

We refer to our letter dated .... in which we confirmed that your tender was not successful. We promised to send you the full list of tenderers and tender prices, and we now list these below. There is, of course, no correlation.

Tenderers

(in alphabetical order)

....

....

....

Prices

(in descending order)

£ ....

....

....

Minimum financial thresholds – public sector: 1 January 2010 to 31 December 2011

	Supplies	Services	Works
Entities listed in Schedule 1*	£101,323 (€125,000)	£101,323 (€125,000)	£3,927,260 (€4,485,000)
Other public sector contracting authorities	£156,442 (€193,000)	£156,442 (€193,000)	£3,927,260 (€4,485,000)
Indicative notices	£607,935 (€750,000)	£607,935 (€750,000)	£3,927,260 (€4,485,000)
Small lots	£64,846 (€80,000)	£64,846 (€80,000)	£810,580 (€1,000,000)

* Schedule 1 of The Public Contracts Regulations SI 2006/5 lists central government bodies subject to the World Trade Organization's Agreement on Government Procurement. These thresholds will also apply to any successor bodies.

Bibliography

Achieving Excellence in Construction: Procurement and Contract Strategies (Office of Government Commerce, 2007).

Code of Practice on Access to Government Information (Department for Constitutional Affairs, 1997).

Construction (Design and Management) Regulations SI 2007/320.

Freedom of Information Act 2000 (c. 36)

Lupton, S., Cox, S. and Clamp, H. *Which Contract? Choosing the appropriate building contract* (RIBA Publishing, 2007).

Production information: a code of procedure for the construction industry (CPIC, 2003).

The Environmental Information Regulations SI 2004/3391.

The Public Contracts Regulations SI 2006/5.